When the unthinkable happens...

Be Prepared,

Be Ready!

A guide about how disasters teach us humanity, give us time to pause and change our course.

DON'T FORGET!

Receive your bonus materials by taking a picture of your receipt and sending it to <u>info@ckmsolutionsgroup.com</u>

Coni K. Meyers, LMC, CBLC, CDC

Founder & CEO of CKM Solutions Group

Copyright © 2021 CKM Solutions Group

All rights reserved. Except as permitted under U.S. Copyright Act of 1976, no part of this publication may be reproduced, distributed, or transmitted in any form or by any means, or stored in a database or retrieval system, without the prior written permission of the publisher or author. For permission requests, write to the author at support@ckmsolutionsgroup.com.

What Others Are Saying About This Book:

"There could not be a better time for this book. I believe helping others is the best way for people to grow and to lead. *When the Unthinkable Happens* will help you with both. I believe in it so strongly we have partnered with Coni to help our brokers and agents be prepared practically, physically, and mentally for any type of disaster along with the communities they serve. Coni has a goal to help millions and I believe she will. I hope you are one of them."
    Tami Bonnell
    CEO EXIT Realty Corp International

"Coni Meyers has drawn upon her extensive experience as a FEMA instructor and trainer to write an excellent guide to help consumers and businesses be ready for and recover from a variety of natural and man-man disasters. Her advice, insights, and recommendations are right on target, which makes *When the Unthinkable Happens* the right book, at the right time, for all the right reasons. Since you never know when the next disaster will strike, everyone should keep this book within easy reach."
    Edward Segal
    Author, *Crisis Ahead: 101 Ways to Prepare For And Bounce Back From Disasters, Scandals, And Other Emergencies*

" Coni Meyer's new book, *When the Unthinkable Happens,* should be read by all of us. You never know when you will encounter an emergency. The time to prepare is before the disaster occurs. Coni, covers many pertinent and important subjects like fear and procrastination, taking an inventory of how prepared you are, and how to make plans today so you can be prepared when disaster comes to you. The time to prepare for a disaster is now. Get this book, make your plan, and use your plan when disaster strikes!"

>**Frank DiBartolomeo, DTM, BSEE, MSEE, MIT, CSEP**
>Lieutenant Colonel, USAF (Ret) and President,
>DiBartolomeo Consulting International (DCI), LLC

"Written by a retired FEMA inspector, this book takes the reader through man-made and natural disasters, and the steps that need to be taken in order to prepare for, survive, and recover from these events. Statistics are cited to remind us that these events do happen, and that being prepared is the best way to have the confidence and skill to weather them. A must-read for anyone interested in keeping themselves and their loved ones safe."

>**Sharron Richardson**
>Vice President, Broker Services EXIT Realty Corp International

"In January of 2020, I was just installed into the New York State Association of REALTORS leadership team. Just a couple of months later, we were in a full-blown pandemic. I feel if we have the tools and insight Coni provides, the outcome could save lives. Everyone, can benefit from this book. This is the kind of book that should be read and shared."

>**Jennifer Vucetic**
>Broker/Owner EXIT Realty Empire Associates

This book is dedicated to the AWESOME team that showed up and supported me in launching CKM Solutions Group and the Crisis Knowledge Management Certification.

Their tireless efforts and commitment to the vision of helping reach 30 million people to be better prepared for disasters and other crises have created a movement that will save lives, save property and save money. You know you are doing something right when the right people, the right resources and the right opportunities show up to make something happen that creates legacy.

Thank you Elaine, Fred, Ana, Michelle, George, Dani, Julie, Gary, Debbie, Michael and Tricia for stepping up and helping to make this book, the courses and the designation happen. Without your dedication none of what we have created would be possible. Together we are helping people be better prepared, survive more readily, and recover faster.

All of you have created a legacy that will live on beyond us. Thank you from the bottom of my heart!

Coni Meyers

Table of Contents

Introduction 8

Chapter 1 Fear and Procrastination 11

Chapter 2 Disasters – What Changed? 18

Chapter 3 How Prepared Are You? 22

Chapter 4 Resilience in Disaster 24

Chapter 5 Make Plans Today 30

Chapter 6 Create a Plan 34

Chapter 7 Make a List 38

Chapter 8 Before, During & After Disasters 40

Chapter 9 Leadership 43

Chapter 10 Communication 46

Chapter 11 Disaster Types 50

Chapter 12 Man-Made Disasters 74

Chapter 13 Recovery Services 83

Conclusion 102

About the Author 104

Other Books by the Author 106

Additional Resources 107

Introduction

In March of 2020, we entered a time of isolation, anxiety, stress, and fear as a result of COVID-19. However, it also became a time of renewal and hope with the opportunity to realign our lives. I wish to dedicate this book to the millions worldwide that have lost their lives to this pandemic, and to all who grieve for them.

As a former FEMA inspector and trainer for 7 years, I have witnessed many kinds of disasters including hurricanes, earthquakes, typhoons, fires, floods, tsunamis, and countless others. Although this is my first experience with a pandemic, the one thing that can be said is that the process of preparedness, survival, and recovery is pretty much the same no matter the type of disaster one goes through. There may be some minor differences, but when you are prepared for one you are prepared for most of them. The information you will learn in this publication can be applied to your personal life, business, and/or community.

One of the most important things that I want you to take away from this book is that there are gifts and opportunities to be discovered in the survival and recovery phases of a disaster. I would encourage all of you to read my book, *Crystalline Moments,* to learn how to identify these important moments of clarity and to understand their significance. We all have thoughts, as well as small and large events that happen in life, that can reveal" crystalline moments." COVID-19 is a large event that has affected lives worldwide. We will not know for some time all the gifts and opportunities that it will bring; there is always chaos before the gifts and opportunities reveal themselves. I can assure you that once this disaster is over and the recovery phase begins, you will see the gifts.

Although it was sad to witness the heartaches and challenges disasters brought, it was the self-sacrificing spirit of humanity that made my job rewarding. Post-disaster many ask themselves "why". I believe that such events happen for a reason, to bring humanity closer together. History will tell the whole story of COVID-19, but for now reflect on the kindness, compassion, and love expressed by many while enduring so much. These are the gifts, or "crystalline moments," that continue to be revealed by disasters, including COVID-19.

I am writing this book to equip you with the practical, physical, and mental tools you need when disaster strikes. I have desired to write this book ever since I completed seven years of employment as a FEMA Inspector and trainer. I believe everything happens when it is supposed to and while experiencing so much during this pandemic, it felt like the perfect time to realize this dream.

Your CKM Advisor has access to forms and materials you will need to be prepared, survive, and recover from disasters which they will make available to you.

Coni Meyers

DON'T FORGET!

Receive your bonus materials by taking a picture of your receipt and sending it to <u>info@ckmsolutionsgroup.com</u>

Chapter 1

Fear and Procrastination

Our first discussion revolves around the topic of fear and stress felt when experiencing disasters. All of us experience fear at some point. Fear results from the unknown, and disasters create many unknowns. It is important not to allow fear and the negativity created by it to get in the way of common sense. You must" stay **in the moment**" and set aside the" what-ifs." **STOP WATCHING 24-HOUR NEWS!!!** Yes, you need to be informed, but watching disaster reports 24/7 is counterproductive to good health. With COVID-19, we were told to build our immune systems. Watching continuous news about what is happening increases levels of cortisol and reduces the ability of our immune system to fight back.

Dr. Kelly McDonnigal's book, *The Upside of Stress*, addresses how our view of stress affects us. She states that if we believe stress is harmful to our health, then it will be harmful; however, if we view stress as a challenge then there is no negative effect. An athlete is a good example of controlled stress. When they are about to enter a game with a challenging opponent or team, they do not panic or faint in fear, instead, they channel stress to motivate them to do their best to win.

When it comes to stress caused by disasters, much depends on our mindset. In the emergency management community, they speak about resilience - the resilience of individuals, businesses, communities, infrastructure, and emergency management teams. Having a resilient mindset will keep fear and stress under control. How can you have a resilient mindset? PREPARE! PREPARE! PREPARE!

Take a minute to close your eyes and imagine that suddenly the ground starts to shake violently. What do you do? Or visualize a knock on your door from a law enforcement officer or firefighter telling you that you have 15 minutes to evacuate. What now? Typically, the first thing that happens is your mind goes blank!

In the face of danger, our fight-or-flight response takes over, blocking what should be a cool and collected reaction. "Mindblanking" takes over. Instead of panic, you MUST turn that "fight-or-flight" behavior into" tend-and-befriend." By doing so, you will know what the first and following steps should be. First responders understand the importance of preparation and practice when it comes to maintaining a resilient mindset that will overcome fear.

In emergency management circles, "Preparedness Procrastination" is a common term and one of the biggest problems in dealing with disasters. Statistics on the number of Americans prepared for disasters vary depending on the type of preparedness that is being discussed. According to a 2015 FEMA release, around 60 percent of Americans have no emergency plan in place. That number has not changed a great deal in recent years. Being prepared means that you have an emergency kit, have a plan of what to do when something happens and that you are informed. Know what types of disasters could potentially happen in your area and know how to stay safe.

According to a survey conducted by The Weather Company in 2019, nearly 40% of Americans have experienced severe weather that damaged their homes or made them evacuate, with one in five happening in the last 5 years. Additionally, as reported by *NU Property & Casualty* magazine, the 2017 hurricane season was one of the most active ever, with three category 4 hurricanes. In May 2019, *Security* magazine reported that only 19% of Americans had a family meet-up plan.

Even with all the conversation and hype about being prepared, a survey conducted by Cummins Home Standby Generators determined that 75% of people felt they were not prepared. Fifty-two percent wanted more food and water, 47% wanted items such as flashlights, batteries, and phone chargers, and 66% wished they had backup power for their home. Additionally, 51% of survey respondents experienced significant inconveniences and financial setbacks. Fifty-one percent said they had to leave their home to stay at hotels or with family or friends and 45% of homeowners suffered property damage, with an average cost of $3,743.00.

According to the Centers for Disease Control and Prevention (CDC), 48% of Americans do not have emergency supplies and 44% do not have first aid kits. Fifty-two percent do not have copies of crucial personal documents. When you look at the overall average of how prepared Americans are in all areas of preparedness, the number is incredibly low. When asked about emergency kits many say they don't have a formal kit, but they know what they would put into one. And therein lies the problem – by the time a disaster strikes, it is far too late to put the kit together.

The bottom line is very few Americans have everything in place that will be needed when something does strike. Many survey findings indicate that overall, 15-17% of Americans are prepared. For this book, we will use an average of 16%.

So why is it so difficult for people to be prepared? It is like making a will, people procrastinate because they do not want to think about dying. Even though we all understand that we should be prepared, the idea that a crisis or disaster could happen is overwhelming. In preparing for disasters, it is *necessary* to think about the possibility of a disaster. While living busy lives and handling smaller day-to-day disasters, people put off preparing for something they do not want to "think" about. It is easier to procrastinate than face what needs to be done to be prepared. In emergency management circles there is a name for this problem, "preparedness procrastination."

How many businesses do you think have a disaster preparedness plan? Unless your business is large, only minimal requirements exist. Things like the evacuation of buildings and knowing the location of fire extinguishers are the extent of preparation. In most areas, government requirements for disaster preparedness do not exist.

If you're a business owner, why should you prepare your business for a disaster? According to FEMA, the U.S. Department of Labor, and the U.S. Chamber of Commerce only 40% of small businesses reopen after a disaster. Of those, 25% will close within a year. If small businesses are not able to reopen within 5 days of a disaster, that number that will not reopen their doors jumps to 90%. Similarly, another statistic states that without preparedness plans, 90% of small businesses, even if they do reopen, are gone after 2 years.

Small businesses lose an average of $3,000 per day while closed, while medium-size businesses lose an average of $23,000 per day. Think of the impact on individuals and communities who rely on those businesses. It is critical to be prepared and NOT procrastinate.

DON'T FORGET!

Receive your bonus materials by taking a picture of your receipt and sending it to <u>info@ckmsolutionsgroup.com</u>

Chapter 2

Disasters – What Changed?

Over the past few years, there has been a significant increase in the number of disasters, including their intensity and impact on everyday life for countless numbers. Also, the cost of disasters has risen dramatically in the last five years. Using figures that are adjusted for inflation, when looking at federal disasters that exceed 1 billion dollars in costs, the numbers are staggering. If you look at the average between 1980 and 2020, the average cost was $45.8 billion a year. However, when you look at the five-year average between 2016 and 2020 the average was $121.4 billion. That is more than a doubling of the costs! The three major reasons for the increase:

Exposure - higher development and value at risk for possible loss. We have seen more land development in highly desirable and more expensive coastal areas which come with a higher risk.

Vulnerability - the amount of damage due to the increased intensity of the weather. For example, winds and floodwaters have increased dramatically over the last few years.

Climate change - increased frequency of extreme weather-related disasters.

From 1980 to 2020, the number of annual events costing over a billion dollars (CPI) averaged 7.0. The annual number of events over a billion dollars from 2016 to 2020 was 16.2. That more than doubles the number of events in recent years.

In 2017, the cost of natural disasters was $309 billion. In 2018, three events just alone cost $73 billion: Hurricane Michael in Florida at $25 billion, Hurricane Florence in the Carolinas at $24 billion, and wildfires in California at $24 billion. Until 2020, the most expensive disaster in the U.S. was Hurricane Katrina in 2005 at $162 billion. With COVID-19, the cost is unknown at this time, but it will exceed any disaster the U.S. has ever experienced.

While natural disasters have increased annually, so have man-made disasters. When looking at active shootings and mass killings, 2019 was the deadliest year on record with 41 incidents and 211 people killed. Cybercrime cost was $13 million in 2019, up from $1.4 million in 2018, and the projected cost of cybercrime over the next five years is estimated to be in the trillions. Due to the inadequately maintained electrical infrastructure, power outages are on the rise with the cost to overhaul and modernize estimated to be in the trillions of dollars.

Insurance companies are scrambling to adjust rates following a disaster due to changes in insurance risk profiles. Since laws do not allow insurance companies to base their insurance rates on future losses, insurance companies are collaborating on projects to reduce greenhouse gases that contribute to weather disasters. Many offer incentives to their clients and employees through programs that promote lifestyle changes to decrease greenhouse gases.

After the wildfires in California, in particular The Camp Fire in the Paradise area, insurance companies started pulling out of affected areas. This resulted in the State Insurance Commissioner enacting a regulation that prohibited insurance companies providing coverage in a designated area from leaving after a disaster.

Some insurance companies increased their rates to the point where people could not afford the insurance premium. In some instances, the rates increased as much as 10 times. After The Camp Fire, one insurance company, Merced Fire and Casualty, had to be liquidated to take care of the claims.

Some scientists are saying that if something is not done to address what is happening, it may reach the point where ordinary people will not be able to afford insurance.

Hopefully, the information presented thus far will move you to protect yourself, your family, your business, and your community.

Chapter 3

How Prepared Are You?

Being prepared will, potentially, save your life and reduce the cost of recovery. The three components to being prepared for disasters are the *why*, the *what*, and the *when*.

When you understand the *why*, you will find the starting point for being prepared. You will also understand the importance of having a resilient mindset and how it will affect the outcome when a disaster strikes. Additionally, you will understand how being prepared helps you react immediately as well as the importance of being self-sufficient, as it may take 24-48 hours before first responders can reach you.

What do you need to have to be prepared? It starts with the basics - your emergency kits and your plans. Having a list of everything you need to take and understanding how important it is to pay attention to emergency alerts is critical. Once you have the basics, you then can look at what additional items should go into the kits depending on the disaster risks in your area.

When to prepare? ***BEFORE*** a disaster, not while the disaster is happening. This *will* save lives. It has been proven that those that are prepared will recover much more quickly than those that are not.

Where do you start? **Mindset!** When you ask victims of disasters and first responders, they will tell you the most important component of ***preparing to survive and recover*** from a disaster is your mindset. "I will be prepared, and I will recover." Your mindset is what keeps you from being disoriented and immobile. A resilient mindset is most important as it not only allows you to bounce back but bounce back better than before the disaster happened.

Chapter 4

Resilience in Disaster

In an interview, Dr. Alia Crum, Assistant Professor of Psychology at Stanford University, explained how a mindset is a lens through which you view the world. The mindset we choose plays a dramatic role in shaping the psychological and physiological effects on attention, arousal, motivation, and affect. There are many types of mindsets: resilient, stressful, challenging, survival, fixed, growth, and persistence to name a few. When it relates to disasters, a resilient mindset is by far the most important.

In emergency management circles, the resilience of communities, businesses, and individuals is a hot topic. First responders will tell you that the most important factor, as it relates to how one prepares, survives, and recovers from a disaster depends entirely on a person's mindset. Resilience is defined as 'the ability to recover quickly from difficulty'.

Why is a resilient mindset so important when it comes to disasters? Usually, the first thing that happens in an emergency is that the mind goes blank, it figuratively freezes. When we believe we have an intruder in the house or that our car has been stolen, we ask ourselves, "What do I do now?" Fear and panic can take control and a person will go into a fight-or-flight response.

One of my interviewees from my 'Kickbutt Leadership Interview Series' has a real estate office with 40 agents in Malibu, California. She was born there, and her mother still lived in their family home. During the Malibu wildfires in 2017, her mother's home was burned to the ground. Many of her agents also had homes that were damaged or destroyed.

She, along with her husband and two little girls, lived a short distance from her mom. Her family got a knock on the door and when she answered it was a fireman letting her know that she and her family had only 15 minutes to evacuate. Mind you, this is a highly intelligent, confident businesswoman. She closed the door and hit the panic button. She spent 5 minutes spinning in a circle trying to figure out what to take. She and her family arrived at the shelter only to discover that they had not brought anything for her girls. As I was talking with her, it was clear that this still caused her anguish.

During a conversation with a Los Angeles Police Chief, who headed up the Community Emergency Response Team (CERT), a training program for volunteers in communities that provides hands-on practical training, he shared with me that he found it difficult to remain in control when he learned that a fire was headed towards his neighborhood. It was his training and resilience that helped him to overcome his fear and be able to perform effectively.

When prepared with a plan, you will know what to do and where you should go. Without preparation there is chaos. With preparation there is resilience. Take a brief look at what happened when COVID-19 spread into the U.S. There was a run-on toilet paper, hand sanitizer, water, and food supplies. Most American's were not prepared, and panic ensued.

In emergency management, resilience means more than "bouncing back." It means re-evaluating plans after a disaster and determining what needs to change to mitigate or lessen the risk of a future disaster. It means rebuilding better than before. A resilient mindset will ask, 'How can we reduce the risk? How can we do a better job of building back?'

Resilient preparedness is planning and training. Resilient survival is responsiveness and efficiency. Resilient recovery is the ability to see a better outcome and rebuilding better than before.

How do you build a resilient mindset when it comes to preparing for the unknown? Here are six tips to embrace resiliency. By following these tips, you will turn resilience into a mindset for change.

S.T.O.P. An acronym used in emergency management: Stop, Think, Observe, and Plan. Jon Kabat-Zinn, the creator of the Stress Reduction Clinic and the Center for Mindfulness in Medicine, Health Care and Society at the University of Massachusetts Medical School, also developed a similar mindfulness practice called S.T.O.P. Stop what you are doing - Take a few breaths - Observe what is happening - Proceed with a plan. By practicing S.T.O.P., you create focus and remain centered, thus allowing you to become resilient.

Stop and take 1-2 minutes to breathe. This allows your mind to clear and identify what needs to be done.

Take decisive action! Once you enact the plan, move forward with confidence. Resilience leads to persistence.

Celebrate your successes. If you are in preparation, celebrate that your emergency kit and plans are complete. If in survival mode, celebrate that no one was hurt or that you survived, and that your home or other possessions can be replaced or rebuilt.

See the beauty. I call life-changing moments "crystalline moments." Crystalline means sparkly or clear, so moments of clarity. In any "crystalline moment" there is always a gift or opportunity. Look around you and find the gift or opportunity in your situation.

Believe that you can recover. Create a vision for the outcome, and the vision will become reality. You cannot go towards a vision, you must come from the vision, and to come from a vision, you must become the vision. By creating a vision, along with having a resilient mindset, you will succeed.

A resilient mindset is important in any scenario. It can mean the difference between being prepared and panicking or making serious mistakes. In survival mode, it may make the difference between surviving or not. In recovery, it is the difference between recovering quickly or not at all. Preparation is key to a resilient mindset, and a resilient mindset is key to success.

Chapter 5

Make Plans Today

The month of September is National Preparedness Month. By having a disaster preparedness plan, you will know what you need to do, how you need to do it and when you need to do it, if and when the time comes.

First, the emergency kit. You need to have a kit for your home, car, and work/business locations. In addition to your regular emergency kit, you need to have a small bug-out bag or BOB. It should only contain essentials in case there is not enough time or space to take your full kit. For example, when being rescued by boat you cannot take a full-size duffle bag. Be sure to include medications, a change of clothes, or whatever essentials are necessary for you.

The basic items in an emergency kit are pretty much the same for each kit, whether it is for the home, car, or work; however, there may be a few items that are different for each kit. And do not forget some *cash*! One of the things that are easily overlooked is putting cash in a kit. Think about how much cash you will need. Imagine if the ATMs are not working, or the electricity is out, and you cannot get cash from a store. It is important to put enough cash into the kit so that you can take care of necessities.

Other items to consider are your photos. When I was doing FEMA inspections, people often related that losing their photos was the most difficult material loss. First, do not store photos on the floor. So many people put pictures in boxes and then either store them on the floor in a closet or under the bed. In the event of a flood, they will be irreparably damaged or destroyed. If you have ever lost pictures from a smartphone, you know how devastating it is. Second, digitize them and either store them on an external hard drive or upload them to the cloud. I suggest, if you can, keeping your external hard drive and/or vintage photos with the emergency kit so that they go with you in an evacuation.

Another consideration is any heirloom items that you could not live without. If the item is too big to put in the emergency kit, plan what you are going to do with these items to make sure they remain safe during a disaster.

One of the first disasters I worked on was a flood in central California. I pulled up to the front of a home and an elderly man was sitting on his front steps weeping. He was holding what appeared to be just a bunch of old wood. When I asked him about the wood, he shared with me that the pieces of wood had been his grandfather's toolbox. Preparing will move you to a plan to protect those items.

Items to have in an emergency kit include:
- Cash
- Water - 1 gallon per person for 3-5 days
- Food - Non-perishable food for 3-5 days, including infant formula and pet food
- Battery-powered radio or NOAA weather radio
- Flashlight and whistle
- Documents - family and other important papers (copied and stored in the cloud)
- Dust masks, plastic sheeting, and duct tape
- Moist towelettes, trash bags, and plastic ties for personal sanitation
- A few basic tools (pliers, screwdriver, wrench, etc.)
- Local map, paper, and pen

- Cellphone with charger, car charger, solar charger, and/or portable power bank
- Prescriptions and an extra pair of glasses
- Fire extinguisher, stormproof matches
- Emergency reference material obtained from the local planning office
- Sleeping bags, clothing, sturdy shoes
- Household items, such as paper supplies, bleach, and a medicine dropper
- Feminine hygiene products or other special needs for household members such as diapers for infants
- Games, books, puzzles

Be sure to evaluate the specific needs of those in your household, especially older adults, and people with disabilities. Once your home kit is complete, focus on creating an emergency kit for your car, and then workplace or business. Once a year be sure to refresh your emergency kits. Take out items with an expired date or that are no longer necessary and replace items that were borrowed from the kits.

Chapter 6

Create a Plan

Next, it is time to create your plans. There are several different types of plans that need to be considered. Let us start with emergency alerts and warnings. If you have not already signed up to receive these alerts, you should do so.

The Integrated Public Alert and Warning System, or IPAWS, is a national system for local alerting that provides authenticated emergency alert and life-saving information messaging to the public through TV, radio, and mobile devices. It was created to unify and modernize the United States' Emergency Alert System, National Warning System, Wireless Emergency Alerts, and the NOAA (National Oceanic and Atmospheric Administration) Weather Radio.

Decide which devices you will have this information on. When a disaster is imminent, you will be given instructions on what to do.

Now, ask yourself:

- What are the special needs of my family?
- What is my parent plan?
- What is my kid plan?
- What is my shelter plan?
- What is my pet plan?
- What are my evacuation routes?
- What is my family/household communication plan?
- What is my business emergency plan?
- What is my staff and team member communication plan?

Consider the unique needs of each household member. Some things to consider are prescriptions, special medical devices, glasses, etc.

The parent plan is the plan for each adult in the household. What will you/they do if at home? At work? And what about the kids? Are they at home, school, a babysitter's, or a friend's home? What are they to do in each of those scenarios?

You should also make plans for your pet(s), as most shelters will not accept them. In every disaster, pets are left behind to fend for themselves under dire circumstances. First responders spend countless hours rescuing these helpless family members. And hundreds of others work to provide food and shelter for them. As an inspector, it was heartbreaking when animals were found. I implore you, **PLEASE DO NOT LEAVE YOUR PETS BEHIND!** Make sure that they have their kit and that you know where they are going.

Often, as in the example of my friend in Malibu, you only have minutes to leave. Learn where the nearest shelter is located so that you are not in the dark as to where to go. If you are at work, know where the closest shelter is, too. The same goes for your family members. If you are separated, everyone needs to know where the closest shelter is that they need to go to. Do practice drills, driving to the shelter using a couple of different routes. It is important to have at least 2 routes you can take. You will learn how to get there and how long it will take.

In Santa Barbara, CA, there is one main route out of town – Highway 101. During their notorious wildfires, the southbound lane was closed for a time because of an overturned truck. It is important to know another route to get out when you need to leave.

This book does not go into detail about a business emergency and continuity plan. If you own a business, the most important thing to have been a communication plan for your staff and team. Create a call tree for your business and decide who is going to call whom. To prepare your business, we recommend visiting www.ready.gov/business.

Once you have created your plans, the next MOST IMPORTANT thing to do is PRACTICE! PRACTICE! PRACTICE! Run drills with the entire family and/or business a minimum of twice a year. Review the plans once a year to make sure that they are up to date.

Chapter 7

Make a List

Make a thorough list of the inventory in your kit so that when you review the kit you know exactly what should be in it. For example, photos, pet information, and heirlooms including what is to be done with them if you cannot take them. Your list should include your plans and important documents organized in a way that makes it is easy to grab and run. Do not forget to make copies and put them on an external hard drive or in the cloud.

Some of the documents you should have copies of include:

- Driver's licenses
- Deeds
- Wills
- Insurance records
- Medical records
- Passports
- Social Security cards

- Birth certificates
- Personal contacts
- Family immunizations
- Pets' medical records
- Home inventory

When a disaster strikes your home or business, whether it is for insurance or taxes, you will need a complete inventory with photos and/or receipts. I can promise that you will not remember everything you own. *IMPORTANT!* Take videos of the inside and outside of your home. Go room by room, with cabinets and drawers open so you have documentation of everything that you owned. Items not covered by insurance may be assessed for special tax deductions.

Chapter 8

Before, During & After Disasters

BEFORE - put your kits, plans, and lists together. *Next* - run family and business drills; if feasible, create a minimum of two ways to get out of each room. Drive evacuation routes so the entire household knows the routes. Maintain and upgrade your emergency kits and plans on an annual basis. Know your company's disaster plan.

NOW - practice **S.T.O.P.** Stop, Think, Observe, and Plan. Stop, take 3 breaths to gather your thoughts. Think, what is your current situation. Observe, what you are feeling (your *inner* voice is telling you what needs to happen next). Plan, you made them and now it is time to use them. Are there any changes needed based on your practice? If so, make the necessary changes to your plan.

DURING - *first*, <u>stop and take 3 deep breaths to center yourself and stay calm.</u> Now is when the planning and practice kicks in, and resilience follows which negates panic. Gather your emergency kits and plans, and do what you are told to do by the authorities. ***Do Not*** put yourself, your loved ones, volunteers, and first responders at risk. As a former FEMA inspector, I can promise you it is not worth it! Help your family to **S.T.O.P.** so that they are present and not paralyzed. If you need to find shelter, do that before anything else.

During the Santa Barbara wildfires, people were told to evacuate, and most did. The fires were put out and residents returned to their homes. A few days later some were told again to evacuate due to the potential of mudslides while others were recommended to evacuate. Some refused to follow that directive resulting in the death of twenty-nine people, three of whom were never found. The name for this phenomenon is "Evacuation Fatigue". **IT CAN NOT BE EMPHASIZED ENOUGH THAT WHEN TOLD TO EVACUATE JUST DO IT!**

AFTER - Secure your property as best you can. If there is damage, do **not** begin clean-up or remove anything until you take photos of what is broken or destroyed, and save **all** expense receipts to present to the insurance adjuster. If there is something unsafe or critical that needs to be removed, then do that after you take a photo. Once your situation is stable, contact all the appropriate agencies for help. In an upcoming chapter, I will provide the many different resources available to help you prepare, survive, and recover from disasters.

Chapter 9

Leadership

What is disaster leadership? It is the difference between a speedy recovery and one that is difficult. In a household and a business, each person should be evaluated for their strengths and weaknesses to determine what role each person will play. Certain skill sets are critical when it comes to disasters and leadership. If you are someone who panics easily, finds it difficult to be decisive or solve a problem, then you may not be the right person to take charge.

It is important to be a good observer of yourself and those around you who may be feeling traumatized or highly charged emotionally. It is critically important to identify those individuals and address their needs as soon as possible.

Author Stephen King says, "There is no harm in hoping for the best as long as you are prepared for the worst." In a disaster situation, this is an absolute truth. The person taking charge will determine what changes may be needed in the recovery phase and make good solid decisions based on the situation.

They will start with where they are, what they have right now and move forward from there. They will determine the first step that needs to be taken, then they will take that step.

Leadership With Children

Time to talk about how children are affected and what can be done to make things less stressful for them. Know that it is ***not*** the words you speak but the body language and tonality being used that will have the greatest impact.

In the planning phase, have an authentic conversation with them about what might happen. Let them be a part of the planning. During a disaster, stay calm so they too will stay calm. Allowing them to help with the preparation will give them a better understanding of what is going on and what comes next. If everything is shared, much of the fear will be minimized. If you need to evacuate, let them bring a personal item that will give them comfort and make them feel safe, such as a teddy bear or blanket.

Be careful of what you say to others if children are present because what they are hearing may be understood differently than what you mean. Be present and available for them.

Frequently ask them questions to find out what they are thinking and feeling. This is especially important once the recovery has started. If children act out, are not sleeping or eating, it may be important to seek professional help for them. When you allow children to be a part of planning and recovery, they are less worried about the future.

Leadership With Your Business

Perhaps you have a thriving business with over 100 employees. Your company is incredibly successful because of your leadership skills that support your team in their sales and marketing efforts. The leadership skills that helped you become successful may not be the leadership skills that are needed in a disaster. You are more likely good at relationship building (which is important in a disaster), but your organizational and project management skills may not be quite as developed. In that case, someone else within your organization should be assigned the leadership role during disasters. A swift recovery comes down to rolling out the plans, making the adjustments, and staying on track with what needs to be done.

Chapter 10

Communication

Communication is KEY in a disaster and is another component of a speedy recovery. A strong communication plan is critical. Everyone in the household and/or business must understand the communication plan. Create a call tree and practice the communication plan so that everyone understands their responsibilities.

Everyone should have an accurate, updated list of all necessary phone numbers and they should know who they will need to call. Make sure to have contacts outside of your area in case communication is down. Having family or friends that everyone can call is vital if you are not able to reach one another.

Involve your children so they understand the importance of being prepared. All children should learn how to call 911 and relate their emergency. Keep a list of updated, all-important phone numbers on the refrigerator or other conspicuous spot so they are prepared to call for help. Have a list in their backpacks or cell phones in the event they are at school or someone else's home. Run family drills to practice the communication plan. Have an intermediary, a relative or friend, outside your immediate area that everyone in the emergency area can call to relate information regarding their safety and well-being.

If evacuated, communicate to others where you will be located. The reverse is also true, when you leave the shelter to return home, make sure to let others know that you are returning. Include a solar charging unit or portable power bank in your kit to maintain communication with others. Be prepared with battery-operated radios to listen to instructions from authorities.

When communicating with one another, be as present as possible so everyone remains calm and stress-free. Researchers have found that approximately 90% of us are not good listeners. When it comes to disasters, listening skills are critical. Listen to instructions from authorities, listen to one another carefully so things are heard correctly, and listen to your children carefully to understand their needs. Watch their body language and tonality to pick up on anything that they may not be saying but that could be a warning sign. Allow children to communicate with grandparents or others they love which will aid in their return to normalcy.

Listening is more than hearing words; it is about paying attention to what is **not** being said. Communication is 55% body language, 38% tonality, and 7% spoken word. Our minds are usually thinking about what we are going to say before the other person has finished, or about something entirely different than what is being conveyed. When it comes to disasters, listening can be the difference between surviving and perishing.

Here are 10 steps to good listening:

Step 1: Face the speaker and maintain eye contact

Step 2: Be attentive, but relaxed

Step 3: Keep an open mind

Step 4: Listen to the words and try to picture what is being said

Step 5: Do not interrupt or impose your "solutions"

Step 6: Wait for the speaker to pause before asking clarifying questions

Step 7: Ask questions only to ensure understanding

Step 8: Try to feel what the speaker is feeling

Step 9: Give the speaker regular feedback

Step 10: Pay attention to what is *not* said

Chapter 11

Disaster Types

Disasters can be classified as natural or man-made. Their impact on countless lives can be catastrophic, not just physically but also mentally. Many individuals who experience a disaster develop post-traumatic stress disorders and depression. It is estimated that as many as 50% of people experiencing a major disaster will require some form of clinical psychological care. The overwhelming loss can leave people too paralyzed to do anything.

Economically, it may be almost impossible to recover. The environmental impact may alter ecosystems and change the livability of an area. The cost of insurance may be unaffordable or not available. Preparedness for each potential disaster is the answer to mitigating as much risk as possible.

Disasters of all types have a major effect on property values. Having multiple types of disasters in a short period can have a lasting effect on market values. Homes located in areas of repeated fire or flooding will experience serious devaluation.

There may be rezoning that will reduce the size of the property or the ability to rebuild at all. Coastline properties that may have an increased risk of flooding, landslides, or storm damage will not be as desirable as they once were.

Following a disaster, appraisers are called upon to determine the value of a partially damaged or destroyed home. Even if a home is not impacted by a disaster, the value can be greatly impacted due to the surrounding damage. It is difficult to find comps for such a neighborhood. How do you figure the value of a home that no longer exists?

Insurance also plays a factor in home values. Many homeowners are forced into foreclosure because of <u>inadequate insurance</u>. According to Frank Nothaft, Executive, Chief Economist for CoreLogic®, "The disruption of a family's regular flow of income and payments, as well as substantial loss in property value, can trigger mortgage default; especially if homeowners are underinsured and cannot afford to rebuild."

Climate change has impacted the real estate industry in profound ways, and it will continue to affect the safety and property values as global warming increases. As a consumer, it is important to understand the effect climate change has on our communities and surrounding areas. It is wise to know what questions to ask when purchasing a home. The following statement is from the article, "Selling Real Estate in the Era of Disaster", from the March 7, issue of *REALTOR® Magazine*. "This year (2019), January's polar vortex caused 60-degree temperature swings from one day to the next in parts of the Midwest, which can be detrimental to homes' plumbing, electrical, and other systems. The new reality is that the country must contend with increasingly violent climate events, and practitioners who live and work in disaster-prone areas are likely to experience more disruption to their transactions."

Once there is a disaster in an area, the ability to obtain a mortgage becomes more difficult due to possible mitigations of future disasters. Insurance rates go up or may not be available. In 2005, the number of low-risk area home values increased by 6.6%, and in 2015 values increased by 9.5%. In 2005, the number of high-risk homes increased by 2.5%, and 6.4% in 2015. High-risk areas are typically in desirable locations such as the west and southwest areas of the United States. It all goes back to community mitigation and preparation to lower the impact that potential disasters may have on any given area. To completely understand the risk, get involved with your community and participate in the preparation.

In this book, I will be covering the following types of disasters: house and wildfires, floods, earthquakes, hurricanes, landslides and mudflows, winter storms, tornados and summer storms, and droughts. CKM Solutions Group offers an online course that goes into a lot more detail about all the natural disasters and more recommendations on preparing, surviving, and recovering from disasters. There is a link at the end of the book.

In considering natural disasters, we will start with understanding the difference between a weather watch and a warning.

Watches are issued 6-12 hours before a severe weather situation. They typically cover a wide area that is prime for severe weather. They have the potential to damage property, as well as threaten the lives of people. Have a plan in case the watch develops into a warning.

Warnings are issued when severe weather is imminent or is already occurring. Typically, they cover a smaller area and last for short periods, approximately 30-60 minutes. ***Take immediate cover or action***.

Each type of threat has its criteria to meet the term "severe," but in all disasters keep your updated and stocked emergency kit close at hand.

At the point of evacuation, no matter what kind of disaster it is, when told to leave do not ask questions and do not discuss with your neighbors whether they are going… just **DO IT**. People lose their lives because they refuse to evacuate. In virtually every disaster, first responders and volunteers put their lives at risk to save those that thought they could outwit Mother Nature.

You may have heard this story: A man received an alert that a river was about to spill over and flood his town and that people should evacuate. He assured himself and said, "I'm a religious man. My God will save me." As the waters rose and started covering the first floor, a boat of rescuers came by to take the man to safety. But the man replied, "I'm a religious man. My God will save me." As the waters continued to rise, the man sought out safety on the roof. Shortly after, a helicopter came hovering overhead and a rescuer shouted down, "I'm dropping this ladder and will take you to safety." For the second time, the man replied, "I'm a religious man. My God will save me." The waters continued to rise, and the man drowned. Standing before his god, he said, "I'm a religious man. I thought you would save me. Why did this happen?" His god replied, "I sent you an alert, a boat, AND a helicopter. What more did you expect?"

PLEASE LEAVE WHEN YOU ARE TOLD.

House Fires

In as little as 30 seconds, a small flame can turn into a major fire. In five minutes, a residence can be engulfed in flames. It takes only a few minutes for a home to fill with black smoke and toxic gases which can cause disorientation and drowsiness. Death by asphyxiation exceeds burns by three-to-one. Save your local fire department's emergency number on your cell phone. Be sure to create an escape plan, especially one to address the evacuation needs of older adults and people with disabilities.

Whether it is your home or business, practice fire drills to ensure that everyone knows how to get out of the building quickly. These drills should include *feeling* your way out and include two exits from each room. If there are screens on the windows, everyone should know how to get them off quickly. If on a second story or higher, how will someone get out of the window safely? Establish two locations where everyone is to meet once they are safe. Make sure to include children in your drills. Have them listen to the fire and carbon monoxide detectors so they know what to do if it goes off.

If your clothes catch fire, **DO NOT RUN!** *Drop* to the ground, *cover* your face with your hands, and *roll* over and over until the fire is out. If you cannot drop and roll, wrap yourself in a blanket or towel to smother the flames. Use cool water (not cold) to immediately treat a burn as the heat will continue to cook the flesh. Cover with a clean dry cloth and seek medical treatment right away. Everyone must know to STOP, DROP and ROLL if their clothes catch fire.

Check your fire and carbon monoxide detectors frequently to make sure they are functioning properly. Fire detectors should be replaced every 8-10 years and batteries tested monthly. Replace the batteries annually unless using non-replaceable 10-year lithium batteries. There should be smoke detectors on every level of the house, especially inside and outside of bedrooms.

During a fire, dark toxic smoke accumulates first at the ceiling; therefore, crawl low and under this cloud. Before opening a door, feel the knob and door to see if they are hot. If they are, use your second escape route to get away. If you cannot get to someone needing assistance, get out and call 911 and tell them where the person is located. If pets are trapped, let the firefighters know right away. If unable to exit a burning building, close the door and cover the vents and cracks around the doors with wet blankets or towels, or other cloth material, to keep gases out. Call 911 and let them know where you are. Go to a window with a cloth or a flashlight to signal where you are. If there is more than one window in the room, keep the other windows shut except the one where you are signaling for help. If in an office building or high-rise, **DO NOT USE AN ELEVATOR!**

Before a fire or other disaster, provide information to your local fire station about any older adults or people with disabilities, and what their needs may be. Be sure to include their location in the home.

Wildfires

Wildfires can flare up and travel quickly. They can move up to 6-14 mph, which can be faster than the average person who runs 10mph. It is critical to be prepared if you live in an area with a potential risk. Sign up for your community's emergency alert system on your cell phone. Know your local evacuation routes and have at least two ways to escape. Do not forget your emergency kit, which should include N95 respirator masks, your pets, and your pet's emergency kit.

Remove flammable materials, debris, and dead vegetation within 100 feet of your property. If you have grass, immediately clean up trimmings after mowing. Use fire-resistant materials when building, renovating, or making repairs to your home. Look at the possibility of retrofitting the roof and siding with fire-resistant materials. Keep important documents in a fireproof box with backup copies stored on an external hard drive and in the cloud. **Review your property insurance with your insurance agent to make sure you are properly covered.** According to insurance industry experts, about 60% of all homes are underinsured.

When the authorities tell you to evacuate, **DO SO IMMEDIATELY!** If trapped, call 911 to let authorities know where you are and then **turn on all lights** so they can find you. A response may be delayed or even impossible, which is why it is so critical to evacuate when you are told to. *No property is worth your life or that of your loved ones.*

Floods

Of all disasters, floods are the most common. They account for 90% of natural disasters and occur in 98% of all U.S. counties. Flooding is defined as rising water and is **NOT** covered by homeowner's insurance. Only water coming from the sky is covered by a homeowner's policy. If you live in an area classified as a flood zone, you are required to carry flood insurance. If you live in a low- to moderate-risk area for flooding, you **can** purchase flood insurance; however, know that 25% of low to moderate-risk areas will experience repeated flooding.

If you experience a natural disaster and receive money from FEMA for flood damage, then flood insurance will be required in the future for that location. During my time with FEMA, I saw numerous floods in small towns near the top of the mountains.

With climate change, the effect of flooding from dangerous storms, tornadoes, and hurricanes is on the rise. FEMA continuously updates its flood maps for at-risk areas. You may not have originally lived in a floodplain, but you may now Check with your local planning office for information about your area. You may want to investigate purchasing flood insurance even if you are not at high risk.

While monitoring for an emergency flood, prepare your home by lifting possessions off the floor and turning off utilities, including electricity, water, and gas. Put sandbags in the toilet and drain hoses to prevent sewage backflow. If there is time, move vehicles, outdoor equipment, chemicals, and toxins to higher locations. Know your plan for older adults and people with disabilities, as well as pets. When you are under a flood warning, evacuate to your shelter immediately.

If it is too late to leave, first and foremost stay calm. Remember to **S.T.O.P.** and say, "I am/We are safe," or whatever you want the outcome to be.

Do not drive into water of an unknown depth! Cars can float in as little as one foot of water, and two feet of rushing water will carry away an SUV and a pickup truck. If your car is flooded, get onto the roof of the car.

Most emergency procedures follow a similar pattern - know your evacuation routes, grab your emergency kit, and find a safe shelter as soon as possible. During floods, do not walk, swim, or drive through floodwaters, and stay off bridges that cross over fast-moving water. Also, avoid drains and waters that are over a knee-deep (use a stick to check depth). Move to higher ground or a higher floor, including the roof of your house until help arrives; however, **NEVER SEEK SHELTER IN AN ATTIC.**

Do not use gas or electrical appliances that have been in floodwater until they have been inspected. Boil tap or other unpotable water until authorities have said it is safe to drink.

Earthquakes

According to research by Statista, between 1974-2003, 42 states had strong naturally occurring earthquakes of a magnitude of 3.5 or higher. Sixteen of those states had twenty or more, with Alaska having the most at 12,053. California came in second with 4,895. (Published by Statista Research Department, and Jun 7. "United States - Number of Strong Earthquakes by State." *Statista*, 7 June 2012, www.statista.com/statistics/203956/number-of-strong-earthquakes-in-the-us-by-state/.)

Studies are currently being conducted to differentiate natural earthquakes from man-made ones. Earthquakes from hydraulic extracting, known as fracking, involve shooting water, sand, and chemicals under high pressure deep into the ground to release oil and gas, which can trigger the movement of faults. Since 2008, there has been a 70% increase in earthquakes in Oklahoma, leaving scientists to believe it is unlikely that all are from natural causes.

There are many things you can do to protect yourself, others, and your property from damage caused by earthquakes. You can secure heavy objects, cabinet doors, framed photos and art, books and bookcases, mirrors, electronics, filing cabinets, water heaters, refrigerators, and other heavy appliances. During an earthquake, **Drop, Cover and Hold on.**

Drop to your hands and knees. Cover your head and neck with arms and, if a table or desk is nearby, go underneath it for shelter. If under a table or desk, hold on with one hand. Do **not** run outside where trees or power lines may fall. Do **not** rely on a door frame. If seated and unable to drop to the floor, bend forward, use your arms to cover your head and neck, and hold until the shaking stops.

DO NOT USE ELEVATORS!

Hurricanes

While there is a debate on whether the annual number of hurricanes is on the rise, it does appear that the intensity and destruction of hurricanes have increased. In 2020, the National Oceanic and Atmospheric Administration (NOAA) predicted a 60% increase in Atlantic hurricane activity this season.

The Atlantic hurricane season is from June 1st to November 30th. The eastern Pacific hurricane season is from May 15th to November 30th. Forecasts for each season are released in May, which is also Hurricane Preparedness Month. Each year, FEMA has a 7-Day Preparedness Plan for the hurricane season, a perfect reminder to review your preparedness. Know your risk, sign up for the emergency alert system, evaluate your emergency kit and have your plans and documents ready, including extra cash. Keep a full tank of fuel in your vehicle or fully charge your electrical vehicle. Start monitoring the alerts at least 36 hours before the hurricane is to make landfall and stay informed regarding evacuation orders. You may want to investigate having a safe room built that meets FEMA guidelines that will withstand strong winds and is high enough to avoid a storm surge.

The best source for hurricane information for the season is your local area's emergency management office and emergency alert center. They will issue updates on what needs to be done if a hurricane is heading your direction.

If sheltering in place, prepare for high winds and flood. Stay on the lowest floor that will not flood and go to an interior wall away from windows. **Do not forget your pets if you are sheltering in place.**

DO NOT SEEK SHELTER IN AN ATTIC AND IF TOLD TO EVACUATE, DO IT!

Landslides and Mudflows

Landslides and mudflows occur throughout the U.S. and its territories resulting from earthquakes, storms, volcanic eruptions, and fires. They may also be caused by development or modifications to the land. The wildfires in Santa Barbara destroyed plant life that had secured the soil from erosion, resulting in huge landslides and mudflows from rain that soon followed. It is not necessarily the amount of rain as it is the rate at which the rain falls that triggers landslides and mudflows. The potential for landslides and mudslides can last for years after a fire. Understand your potential risk by getting a proper inspection. Once the risk has been evaluated, experts can make recommendations for mitigation. Planting ground cover is one thing that can be done to help reduce the risk, as well as building retaining walls and other diversion systems for water and debris. It is important to know the warning signs for potential problems and to stay tuned to the alerts from authorities.

Extreme Winter Storms

The intensity of extreme winter storms has increased in recent years. If you live in an area where winter storms are frequent, you know the need to properly insulate your home and pipes, and to stay tuned to weather warnings. Before the beginning of the winter storm season, be sure to check your emergency kit and review your plans, including plans in case your home loses power or you are confined to your home. It is also necessary to keep food and water stocked to last for at least seven days. The emergency kit in your car should include what you would need if you found yourself stranded in your car.

Frostbite is common on fingers, toes, the nose, ears, cheeks, and chin. Here are the signs and symptoms:

- Cold prickling feeling of extremities
- Numbness
- Red, white, bluish-white, or grayish-yellow skin
- Hard or waxy-looking skin
- Clumsiness due to joint and muscle stiffness
- Blistering after rewarming

Hypothermia is caused by prolonged exposures to very cold temperatures; whereby, your body begins to lose heat faster than it produces it. Here are the signs and symptoms:

- Blistering after rewarming in severe cases
- Shivering
- Exhaustion
- Confusion
- Fumbling hands
- Memory loss
- Slurred speech
- Drowsiness

Limit the amount of time outdoors and wear layers of clothing when it is necessary to go out. When shoveling outside, **do not over-exhaust yourself.** Stay off the road as much as possible. Do **NOT** use generators, grills, gas stovetops, or gas ovens to heat the house. Each year, an average of 430 Americans die from carbon monoxide poisoning, more than 20,000 require a visit to an emergency room, and more than 4,000 are hospitalized. These numbers increase over the winter months in part because of the misuse of the appliances.

If you have any animals, have a plan to protect them and have plenty of food and water for them.

Tornados and Summer Storms

According to an article in the May 30, 2019, issue of *InsideClimate News,* entitled "Is Climate Change Fueling Tornados?" Penn State University climate researcher Michael Mann said that there is growing evidence that "a warming atmosphere, with more moisture and turbulent energy, favors increasingly large outbreaks of tornadoes, like the outbreak we've witnessed in the last few days." "There is also some evidence that we might be seeing an eastward shift in the regions of tornado genesis—again, consistent with what we are seeing," he added.

(Berwyn, Bob. "Is Climate Change Fueling Tornadoes?" *Inside Climate News*, 30 Nov. 2020, insideclimatenews.org/news/30052019/tornado-climate-change-connection-science-research-data)

Within the same article, Harold Brooks, a senior scientist with the National Severe Storms Laboratory in Norman, Oklahoma, stated that tornadoes are complex, dynamic, short-lived, and small, which makes them hard to study. But the deadly 2011 outbreak, which included the tornado that tore through Joplin, Missouri, spurred a new wave of studies that help explain how global warming affects tornado activity.

Brooks also stated that researchers are looking at severe storm development because even without tornadoes, giant thunderstorms can produce damaging hail and destructive winds. This is a robust signal that global warming will make the atmosphere more likely to spawn such storms.

To be prepared for a tornado, you need to know where you are going to go in your home when a tornado warning is issued. If you do not have a safe room that you can escape to, consider having one built that meets FEMA's criteria. It is important to run drills with children, so they know what to do. Have a plan for your pets so they are not left outdoors. Pay attention to tornado warning signals and what authorities are telling you to do. Make sure you grab your emergency kit to take with you!

If you are in a car, do not attempt to outrun a tornado. Try seeking shelter in a building or underground. If you can safely get much lower than the level of a roadway, get out of the car and lay on the ground in that area with your hands on the back of your head. If there is no significantly lower place, stay in your car with the seatbelt on. Lower your head below the windows and get as low to the bottom of the vehicle as possible. If you have a blanket or jacket, place it over your head and place your hands over your head. You may have heard that it was a good idea to get under an overpass but that is very dangerous and not recommended as the winds from the tornado can blast debris under the overpass.

Drought

Drought preparedness is all about water conservation. Never pour water down the drain if there is something else you can do with it. Almost every part of the U.S. experiences periods of reduced rain. Planning and preparedness during normal rainfall years will equip us for droughts. A few years ago in central California, there were entire towns that ran out of water and had to have water brought in. Doing anything you can to conserve water will help to preserve water for dry times.

Things you can do <u>indoors</u> to conserve water:

- If you have dripping faucets, replace washers or the actual faucets themselves if washers do not fix the problem. Just one drop per second uses 2,700 gallons in a year.
- Check for and repair leaks, and retrofit faucets, showerheads, and toilets with flow restriction devices.
- Insulate pipes to reduce heat loss and prevent them from breaking in freezing weather.
- Place a one-gallon jug of water into the toilet tank to reduce water consumption.
- Choose appliances that are water and energy-efficient.
- Only use water softener systems when minerals will cause damage to pipes.
- Use a compost pile rather than garbage disposal.
- Avoid flushing the toilet unnecessarily, taking long showers or deep baths.
- Do not allow water to run unnecessarily while brushing your teeth, washing your face, or shaving.

- Run the dishwasher only when it is full and use the "smart" water feature, and do not rinse dishes before putting them in the dishwasher.
- Instead of wasting water while you let it get hot or cold, capture water for other uses; otherwise, install an instant water heater or, for cold water, store water in a refrigerator.
- Do laundry only as full loads and use the water conservation feature.

Things you can do <u>outdoors</u> to conserve water:

- Use commercial car washes that recirculate the water.
- Plant native plants or drought-tolerant ground cover, trees, or grasses.
- In drought areas, xeriscape your yard with drought-tolerant plants that require little to no irrigation.
- Group plants together so that you can water multiple plants at the same time with the same water.
- Use mulch to not only controls weeds but also to retain water.

- If you install water features, use circulating water appliances.
- Do NOT purchase water toys that require a constant stream of water.
- Set up a system for saving rainwater. Contact your local water company, as they can give you specific ideas that will work in your area and how to do it.
- If you have a lawn, use an irrigation system that is water efficient and position sprinklers so they are watering just the lawn.
- Be vigilant with leaks and broken sprinkler heads. They should be repaired immediately.
- Look at areas around your lawn where you can eliminate some of the grass and replace it with native shrubs and plants, or consider installing the latest generation of artificial turf.

Chapter 12

Man-Made Disasters

Countless types of man-made disasters occur throughout the world, but for the sake of brevity, only five will be covered in this book - pandemics, active shooters and mass attacks, household chemical emergencies, cyberattacks, and natural gas leaks. CKM Solutions Group offers an online course that goes into a lot more detail about all man-made disasters and more recommendations on preparing, surviving, and recovering from these disasters. The link is at the end of the book.

Epidemics and Pandemic

First, let us discuss the difference between an epidemic and a pandemic. Epidemics are when a disease affects many people in a particular region or country, and is out of control and spreading quickly. As an example, when COVID-19 was prevalent in just China, it was an epidemic. A pandemic is an epidemic that has crossed multiple continents, as we have seen with the worldwide spread of COVID-19.

As mentioned earlier, I am writing this while we are experiencing COVID-19. Most of us watched daily news reports of the hoarding of toilet paper, sanitizers, cleaning supplies, food, and water. Few families were prepared! Your emergency kit should already include these items, making a" run" for them unnecessary. Also, you will need a sufficient supply of prescriptions, nonprescription drugs, and other medical supplies. Know how to access your medical records online and have them secured in a fire- and waterproof safe and saved on an external hard drive or in the cloud.

Over the centuries, millions have died due to pandemics, plagues, or other diseases. According to an article in *National Geographic* magazine, published January 31, 2014, and entitled "Two of History's Deadliest Plagues Were Linked, With Implications for Another Outbreak," it is believed that in the sixth century, 30 to 50 million people died in one year, about half of the world's population, from the Justinianic Plague.

(Berwyn, Bob. "Is Climate Change Fueling Tornadoes?" *Inside Climate News*, 30 Nov. 2020, insideclimatenews.org/news/30052019/tornado-climate-change-connection-science-research-data.)

Smallpox, which has been present for hundreds of years, is believed to have killed 300 million in the 20th century alone. These large events have been reduced in recent years due to modern medicine, protocols, and technology. As of this writing, it is unclear what the final death toll will be for COVID-19. This pandemic has not just affected people, but uniquely the world economy.

To prevent contagious disease and limit the spread of germs, follow these simple protocols:

- Wash your hands completely for 20 seconds with soap
- Avoid close contact (6 feet minimum)
- Wear a mask - cover your mouth and nose
- Avoid touching your face
- Practice other healthy habits such as getting plenty of sleep, being physically active, managing your stress, drinking plenty of fluids, and eating nutritious food

Active Shooters and Mass Attacks

It is unfortunate that this is something we need to discuss; however, in our nation, it has come to be seen as a sign of the times. I live in Las Vegas and on the night of October 1, 2018, we witnessed the horror as 58 people died, gunned down by a lone shooter.

Furthermore, I have a sister and a friend who were in malls when suspicious gunshots occurred. No one was hurt but the fact that I know two people who experienced something that could have been so much worse is very scary.

I am very fortunate that I didn't know anyone that was injured or killed in the shooting in Las Vegas; however, I know several people who know someone that was. That event had a huge effect on everyone that calls Vegas home. There was certainly fear and enormous grief. There was also a huge outpouring of support and love for those that were at the concert and impacted directly by this mass murderer.

An active shooter is defined as an individual actively engaged in killing or attempting to kill people in a populated area. Mass attacks are defined as the murder of 4 or more persons in a single event. These incidents have underscored the importance of a coordinated response by law enforcement and other emergency services.

What can we do to protect ourselves? First, if you *see* something suspicious, *say* something to authorities. When entering a building, identify the exits and make yourself aware of possible hiding places.

Many communities offer courses for active shooter training. If confronted with a shooter, ***RUN*** (they may miss a vital organ or miss you altogether) and try to warn others. If you cannot get away, find a place to hide, such as another room where you should lock and block the doors, turn out the lights and close the blinds. ***Do not*** hide in groups or spread out along walls. Mute your cell phones including the sound from vibration.

Communicate with the police silently through text messaging. Stay where you are until the police let you know it is okay to come out.

The last resort is to fight! Commit to your actions and act aggressively using whatever weapon is at hand: a chair, fire extinguisher, scissors, or books.

Whether you are directly involved in a shooting situation or whether you are in a community where there has been an incident, consider seeking professional help to deal with the emotional trauma. After the shooting in Las Vegas, there were services made available to people living here.

Household Chemical Emergencies

Although the risk of a household chemical emergency is minimal, knowing how to handle hazardous household products can reduce the risk of injury. It is important to store household chemicals in places where children cannot reach them.

Products such as aerosol cans of furniture polish, hair spray, deodorant, and bathroom cleaner are considered hazardous materials. Other items include cleaning products, nail polish and polish remover, pesticides, automotive products, kerosene, lighter fluid, and painting supplies.

Always keep products in original containers and never remove the labels unless you need to change the container because the original is corroded. Never mix household chemicals with other products as incompatibility could cause them to ignite, explode or create toxic fumes. If there is a spill, clean it up immediately, put rags in plastic containers and dispose of them in the trash. If a sizable accident occurs, get everyone out of the house immediately!

Symptoms of poisoning include difficulty breathing and irritation of the eyes, skin, or throat. They also include changes in skin color, headache, blurred vision, dizziness, clumsiness or lack of coordination, cramps, and/or diarrhea.

Add the National Capital Poison Control as a contact on your cell phone: 800-222-1222 - and if someone is experiencing any of these conditions, call their number and follow their instructions implicitly. Discard all clothing that may have been contaminated as many chemicals do not wash out completely.

Cyberattacks

A cyberattack is any attempt to gain illegal access to a computer or computer system to cause damage or harm. This has led to the creation of cybersecurity, which is the art of protecting networks, devices, and data from these unauthorized accesses. Cybersecurity is important to ensure confidentiality, integrity, and availability of information.

What are the risks? Hackers, attackers, or intruders using malicious code and attacking vulnerable areas.

How do you minimize the risk? Keep software up to date, use strong passwords and change them often, use multi-factor authentication, and incorporate firewalls. Be aware of suspicious activity, use secure internet connections, and create backup files.

If an attack happens, take all devices offline, change passwords immediately, and scan and clean the device (you may want to use a professional). Contact banks, credit card companies, and other financial accounts. Additionally, contact credit bureaus and disallow any credit approvals. You should also reach out to the police and Federal Trade Commission, file a report with the Inspector General, and file a complaint with the FBI Internet Crime Center. For online crime, report it to the local Secret Service Electronic Crimes Task Force or Internet Crime Complaint Center.

Natural Gas Incidents

Natural gas explosions happen when there is a leak that ignites. In the U. S., the primary sources of gas are natural and propane gas. Over the years, many have been killed or injured due to gas explosions. In 2019, 659 incidents killed 13 and injured 37 people.

To prevent dangerous incidents with natural gas, install a natural gas detector and regularly test the detector. Locate gas lines before digging by calling 811 or going to call811.com.

Maintain all gas appliances and have them checked regularly. Teach everyone in your household how to shut off the main gas valve. If it becomes necessary to turn the gas off, **DO NOT** attempt to turn it back on. Call a professional to turn the gas back on.

If you smell gas, **get out immediately.** *Do not* use a cell phone, turn on a light or anything electrical, and *do not* light a flame. A fire extinguisher should be on hand.

Chapter 13

Recovery Services

There are many recovery services available depending on the disaster and its impact. However, it would be impractical to list them all here. A brief description and a few websites can easily be found for major ones. These include government agencies, non-profits, and faith-based charities. There are wonderful opportunities to volunteer with some of these amazing organizations.

Federal Emergency Management Agency (FEMA)

The Federal Emergency Management Agency, or FEMA, is one of the agencies within the U.S. Department of Homeland Security (DHS). FEMA was created in 1979 through an executive order signed by President Jimmy Carter. The history of FEMA dates to the Congressional Act of 1803. This was the first disaster legislation.

FEMA's mission is, "Helping people before, during, and after disasters." They are responsible for coordinating the different roles of different governmental agencies, states and regional responses, and other organizations' responses. There are several government agencies and programs that either fall under the FEMA umbrella or work in conjunction with FEMA. They oversee the preparation, prevention, mitigation, and response, and recovery from both natural and man-made disasters. FEMA is called into action when there is a presidentially declared disaster.

In addition, they have individual programs that assist disaster victims. These include mental health and employment programs. Their main program is called Individual Disaster Assistance Program. This program ensures that a home is "safe, secure and sanitary".

To be clear, ***FEMA is not an insurance company!*** FEMA is not there to make someone whole. They provide a flat dollar for items that are required to make a home safe, secure, and sanitary. These include structural items like roofing, foundation, walls, sheetrock, insulation, paint, and systems in the house, such as HVAC systems and water in the house.

They will provide a flat dollar amount to ensure each member of the household has necessities, such as a bed, a chair, and utensils for each household member. Provisions do include the need for a TV, but they will not be replacing your 75" latest model. They provide a flat dollar amount for one TV and radio so that households can stay informed for the sake of safety.

National Flood Insurance Program (NFIP)

This agency, which falls under FEMA, was founded in 1968 to determine the level of flood risk in areas and identify the potential as low-, moderate-, or high-risk. Communities must agree to mitigate and adopt certain control measures to participate in NFIP.

As previously covered, if a property is in a high-risk area, then it is required to carry flood insurance. Low- and moderate-risk areas are not required to obtain flood insurance; however, 25% of these properties will experience flooding. In 2018, 15% of homes had flood insurance. That same year, NFIP showed a deficit of $20.5 million. This has led FEMA to mandated that this program be reviewed overall, including updating floodplain maps.

Community Emergency Response Team (CERT)

The Los Angeles City Fire Department gave birth to this program in 1985. In 1993 it became a national program and a part of FEMA. Since it can take up to 48 hours to get first responders into devastated areas, residents must take care of themselves in these situations.

CERT provides hands-on training for people in a community so they can take care of themselves until help arrives. Each community program is based upon the types of risk the community may face. The training includes light search and rescue, fire safety, team organization, and disaster medical training. The training is free and takes about 17.5 hours to complete. The CERT Program is in all fifty states, in 2,700 communities, and has over 600,000 volunteers.

The U.S. National Response Team (NRT)

Started in 1978, and as part of the then Bureau of Alcohol, Tobacco and Firearms, the U.S. National Response Team was created in response to a significant increase in arson and explosion incidents. Its purpose is to initiate a quick disaster response.

Since its inception, NRT has responded to over 700 incidents. They can respond anywhere in the U.S. within 24 hours. The teams are comprised of veteran agents experienced in the blast and fire origin-and-cause, forensic chemists, fire protection engineers, explosive enforcement officers, and detection canines, as well as legal, intelligence, and audit support. To accomplish the goal of responding within 24 hours 13 Regional Response Teams cover the US states, their territories, and possessions.

National Domestic Preparedness Consortium (NDPC)

Established in 1998, the National Domestic Preparedness Consortium is a FEMA training partner that provides high-quality training for emergency responders. They conduct training in all 50 states and territories. The training has benefited more than 1.9 million people. They have trained more than 60,000 state, local, and tribal emergency responders, and employees.

Centers for Disease Control and Prevention (CDC)

Under the U.S. Department of Health and Human Services (HHS), the Centers for Disease Control and Prevention (CDC) is another government agency that plays a key role in disasters and other health risks. In 1946, Dr. Joseph Mountin founded the then Communicable Disease Center. At the time, Dr. Mountin was considered a visionary public health leader and advocated for public health issues. He paid Emory University a token of $10 for the land in Atlanta that the CDC still sits on today.

The CDC's original function was to prevent malaria from spreading across our country. Its main goal now is to protect public health and safety through the control and prevention of disease, injury, and disability, both in the U.S. and abroad. In addition to dealing with the prevention of disease and establishing protocols during an outbreak, such as Covid-19, the CDC's work is vital when it comes to school health, tobacco use, nutrition, obesity, heart disease, stroke, diabetes, cancer prevention, and control, and many other societal health issues.

Non-profits and Other Organizations

Many organizations do amazing humanitarian work when it comes to disasters. Many were started by one or two people that saw a need. If any of these organizations tug at your heart, reach out and join, they would love to have you.

American Red Cross

Founded by Clara Barton in 1881, the American Red Cross' mission statement is, "The Red Cross, born of a desire to bring assistance without discrimination to the wounded on the battlefield, endeavors—in its international and national capacity—to prevent and alleviate human suffering wherever it may be found." Its purpose is to protect life, health and to ensure respect for the human being. In 2019, 306,000 volunteers responded to 60,047 disasters and incidents and provided 529,430 services.

SBP

The SBP (formerly known as the St. Bernard Project) was founded in 2006 by Zack Rosenburg and Liz McCartney as they volunteered at St. Bernard Parish after Hurricane Katrina. They saw the commitment of the people in the community to rebuild, but also saw the painful slowness of the traditional rebuilding processes. They decided to launch an organization to "Shrink Time".

SBP's mission is to rebuild homes quickly, share rebuilding innovations with other rebuilding organizations to improve the process nationally, help communities to be better prepared, provide advice to policymakers immediately after a disaster to empower them to recover more quickly and advocate for reforms in disaster strategies.

SBP is supported and greatly enhanced by AmeriCorp members and boasts 30,000 volunteers. They are supported by donations, volunteers, and corporate partners.

Americares

In 1975, a U.S. jet carrying 243 Vietnamese orphans bound for the United States crashed in the jungle outside of Saigon. One-third of the children were killed, and others were critically injured. The Pentagon said it would take 10 days for resources to get to these children. Robert Macauley, a paper broker in Connecticut, heard about the accident and chartered a plane that, 24 hours later, brought the remaining children to California.

That was the beginning of Americares. It is now the world's leading transporter of medicine and medical supplies. It operates in over 90 countries and all 50 U.S. states. It provides over $500 million of innovative health programs and medical aid each year. "The only thing that's going to save the world is love. Pure and simple. Just love," said Bob Macauley.

Team Rubicon®

The Haiti earthquake in 2010 put two U.S. Marine veterans, Jake Wood and William McNulty, into action. They gathered supplies, a small group of volunteers (veterans, medical professionals, and first responders), and went to Haiti. They called themselves Team Rubicon (from the phrase "crossing the Rubicon" which is an idiom meaning passing a point of no return) because they knew when they crossed over from the Dominican Republic into Haiti there was no turning back.

This group helped many who other organizations overlooked. They have served thousands of survivors using their military, medical and leadership skills. They are now a global organization with five separate networks in other countries. They provide effective humanitarian aid in the wake of disasters while "serving veterans by serving others." This organization has formed 275 response teams with over 80,000 volunteers.

All Hands and Hearts

Originally two separate non-profits, All Hands Volunteers (founded by David Campbell in 2005) and Happy Hearts Fund (founded by Petra Nemcova in 2005), they came together in late 2017 to form All Hands and Hearts. They enlist volunteers to work directly with community leaders to meet short- and long-term needs within a disaster area. Their method of helping families recover faster is by using their Smart Response strategy. This strengthens both the volunteers and the communities they serve. Over the last 15 years, they have provided disaster relief to more than 1.1 million people around the world.

Doctors Without Borders

In May of 1968, a group of French doctors committed to helping victims of wars and major disasters. They are known as Médecins Sans Frontières, or internationally in English as Doctors Without Borders. These doctors were horrified when for the first time on television, children were seen dying from hunger and war.

Two of these doctors, Max Recamier and Bernard Kouchner, felt it was important for the world to see what was happening in the province of Biafra, which had seceded from Nigeria and was surrounded by the Nigerian army. They traveled to the war zone where hospitals were doing surgery in areas regularly targeted by the Nigerian army. Civilians were also being murdered and starved by the Nigerian army.

Bernard Kouchner had stated, "We wanted to ensure sufficient knowledge of this new type of medicine: war surgery, triage medicine, public health, education, et cetera. It's simple really: go where the patients are. It seems obvious, but at the time it was a revolutionary concept because borders got in the way. It is no coincidence that we called it 'Médecins Sans Frontières.'"

Today, Doctors Without Borders is in 28 countries, employing 30,000 people worldwide, and since 2014 has completed 8.25 million outpatient consultations.

Direct Relief®

After World War II, William Zimdin, a wealthy immigrant from Estonia, started sending thousands of foods, clothing, and medical packages to family, friends, and former employees. He soon dedicated himself to helping the oppressed and established the William Zimdin Foundation in 1948. In 1957, it was renamed Direct Relief Foundation. In 1962, it became licensed as a wholesale pharmacy that developed strict guidelines for the proper types and use of any aid shipments sent to devastated areas.

Their name changed a few more times and, in 2013, they renamed themselves Direct Relief. Their mission is to improve the health and lives of people affected by poverty or emergencies- without regard to politics, religion, or ability to pay, and to serve "disadvantaged populations living in medically under-served communities throughout the world." The qualifications of health professionals and inventories are closely looked at. They are active in all 50 U.S. states and more than 80 countries.

REACT International, Inc

REACT International, Inc. was started by a group of CB radio volunteers to assist motorists in 1962. It expanded to a network of communication professionals dedicated to assisting communities in times of disaster. Their support assists local resources to "accelerate relief efforts".

Extensive programs have been developed for the relationships between the REACT Teams, emergency services, and governments. REACT Teams assist police with public events and traffic control, including providing any special equipment that may be required. Training includes FEMA's required courses for participation in emergency and disaster communications.

ShelterBox

ShelterBox prides itself on thinking" outside the box." They started in Cornwall, England as a millennium project through the Rotary Club. Today, it has become a global organization made up of people who believe in shelter as a human right – that "shelter from the chaos of disaster and conflict is vital."

Where there is a disaster, chaos follows. Losing your home is beyond chaos, as it affects everything you need to do to start the recovery process. ShelterBox promotes stability by reaching out to the most vulnerable in war zone areas like Syria and the Lake Chad Basin.

ShelterBox speeds recovery by providing green box kits with tents, tarps, ropes, nails, tools, and other specific items for rebuilding shelter, depending on where the need is located. They also provide blankets, solar lights, mosquito nets, water filters, containers, and cooking pots. They have helped shelter 1.5 million people in 100 countries since 2000.

UNICEF (United Nations Children's Fund)

Established by the United Nations General Assembly in 1946, UNICEF promotes the rights and well-being of every child. They work in 190 countries and territories to care for the needs of children going through crisis, violence, disasters, and poverty. They promote girls' education, immunizations, the fight against HIV/AIDS, and the protection of children from abuse and violence.

They uphold the four core principles of the United Nations Convention on the Rights of the Child, which include non-discrimination, devotion to the best interests of the child, the right to life, survival, and development, and respect of the views of the child.

NOVA (National Organization for Victims Assistance)

Founded in 1975, NOVA is a recognized leader in victim advocacy, education, and public policy initiatives that protect the rights of crime victims. Their mission: "Champion dignity and compassion for those harmed by crime and crisis." Their work includes advocating for victims by connecting them to resources, and training advocates and crisis responders. They provide support across the country with over 600 NOVA-trained Crisis Responders delivering education and emotional first aid.

Faith-Based Organizations

I want to emphasize that there are hundreds of faith-based organizations that reach out to help victims in times of need. This list is just a sample of a few of them.

The Salvation Army

William Booth, a London minister, took his message to the streets where he ministered to the homeless, the poor, the hungry, and the destitute. The basic services set back in 1878 are still a part of The Salvation Army's mission today. New services have been added to address today's needs in disaster relief. Today, The Salvation Army is in 125 countries.

Volunteers of America®

To provide affordable housing and other assistance to low-income people, Volunteers of America was formed in 1896. There are 32 affiliates who have served 1.5 million people each year. They work with older adults, veterans, families, the homeless, people with disabilities, those addicted to drugs, and those who have been incarcerated. In 2017, VOA owned 19,000 affordable housing units that helped 25,000 people each year.

Samaritan's Purse®

Founded in 1970 by Bob Pierce after visiting suffering children on the Korean island of Koje-do, Samaritan's Purse is a non-denominational Christian organization that helps victims of disasters, wars, poverty, and famine. His mission was "to meet emergency needs in crisis areas through existing evangelical mission agencies and national churches." They provide spiritual, as well as physical help, that includes women's programs, agricultural help, education, clean water, sanitation, and construction.

NECHAMA Jewish Response to Disaster

NECHAMA, which is "rooted in the Jewish value of Tikkun Olam, 'repairing the world,' provides comfort and hope to communities by engaging volunteers in disaster recovery work." Volunteers are trained to assist disaster survivors with cleanup, debris removal, cleaning, and sanitizing homes and repairing homes with sheetrock, insulation, paint, flooring, and more.

Children's Disaster Services

Children's Disaster Services has been helping children since 1980 by setting up childcare centers inside shelters and disaster assistance centers. Their volunteers are professionally trained to work with traumatized children. They go through a rigorous screening process and provide a safe, calm space for the children to heal. Volunteers make their appearance with a "Kit of Comfort," which is filled with special toys that stimulate imagination and encourage children to express their feelings.

Friends Disaster Service

Founded in 1974 after a tornado destroyed Xenia, Ohio, Friends Disaster Service provides volunteers for labor, who bring their tools and expertise. They affect each "community and the world: one person, one family, one project at a time." They provide relief for all survivors but will seek out older adults, people with disabilities, low-income families, and the uninsured. They work with other first responders and focus on rebuilding.

Catholic Charities USA®

In 1910, four hundred people founded Catholic Charities USA "to bring about a sense of solidarity" among church members that work on different charitable ministries, and "to be an attorney for the poor." The mission of Catholic Charities USA is "to provide service to people in need, to advocate for justice in social structures, and to call the entire church and other people of goodwill to do the same." In 1990, an agreement between Catholic Charities USA and the U.S. Conference of Catholic Bishops formally tasked Catholic Charities USA with taking on disaster response efforts. The volunteers are in communities to provide direct relief when disaster strikes and will be in the community for as long as they are needed.

These are just a sampling of the different organizations that are involved with disaster relief efforts. If the mission of any of these organizations draws you to them, please reach out to them directly to see how you can get involved.

Conclusion

Hopefully, you have found this book informative or as insightful as the subject matter of disasters can be. If you begin preparing for disasters in your area now, it will not only make you resilient when something happens but also help you remain calm.

Instead of thinking, "I really need to do this," you can say, "YES, I did it!" Do not let "Preparedness Procrastination" settle in!

One of my favorite stories is by the ancient poet Rumi. He tells the story of a prince coming of age. The king comes to the young man and tells him it is time to go out into the world and gives him one task to accomplish. The prince is gone for a long time which worries the king. The king decides to go in search of his son. When the king finds the prince, he goes on and on about everything he has accomplished. The king asks him if he did the one thing that he had told him to do. The prince replies "No," so the king says, "Then it is as if you have done nothing." For me, the king represents God while the prince is humanity. If we do not go into the world and live our purpose, then it is as if we have done nothing.

Become resilient! Take care of your family, friends, business team, associates, and community. Help others become resilient, as well.

It is my vision and passion to take the approximate 16% statistic of Americans who are prepared for a disaster up to 25%, or 30 million people. This will save a lot of lives and billions of dollars.

Be the one saying "yes" to saving lives.

"Disasters teach us humanity, give us a chance to pause, reflect, and change course."

About the Author

Coni Meyers, LMC, CBLC, CDC, Crisis Management Specialist, and Leadership Clarity Strategist has spent over 40 years supporting thousands of individuals and businesses.

During her seven years as a FEMA inspector and trainer, Coni witnessed many kinds of disasters: hurricanes, earthquakes, typhoons, fires, floods, tsunamis, and countless others. Although this is her first experience with a pandemic, the one thing that can be said is that the process of preparedness, survival, and recovery is pretty much the same no matter the type of disaster one goes through. There may be some minor differences, but when you are prepared for one you are prepared for most of them.

She is an international best-selling author, speaker, and trainer.

Contact and Social Media Information:

Website: ckmsolutionsgroup.com

Email: info@CKMSolutionsGroup.com

Facebook: www.facebook.com/CKMSolutionsGroup

Instagram: www.instagram.com/ckm_solutions_group/

LinkedIn: www.linkedin.com/in/conimeyersckmadvisor/

YouTube: https://tinyurl.com/CKMSgroup

Phone: **800-634-9677**

DON'T FORGET!

Receive your bonus materials by taking a picture of your receipt and sending it to info@ckmsolutionsgroup.com

Other Books by the Author

__Crystalline Moments: Discover Your Opportunities and Create Your Best Self__

__Leadership in Trying Times: Advice to Lead and Succeed__

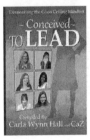
__Conceived to Lead: Dismantling the Glass Ceiling Mindset__

DON'T FORGET!

Receive your bonus materials by taking a picture of your receipt and sending it to info@ckmsolutionsgroup.com

Additional Resources

Department of Homeland Security (www.dhs.gov)

Operational and Support Components within the Department of Homeland Security

- U.S. Citizenship and Immigration Services (USCIS) (www.uscis.gov)
- U.S. Customs and Border Protection (CBP) (www.cbp.gov)
- Federal Emergency Management Agency (FEMA) (www.fema.gov)
- U.S. Immigration and Customs Enforcement (ICE) (www.ice.gov)
- Transportation Security Administration (TSA) (www.tsa.gov)

- United States Coast Guard (USCG) (during times of peace) (www.uscg.mil)
- Cybersecurity and Infrastructure Security Agency (CISA) (www.cisa.gov)

Other agencies that are involved in some phases of disasters

- Central Intelligence Agency (CIA) (www.cia.gov)
- U.S. Department of Agriculture (USDA) (www.usda.gov)
- U.S. Department of Defense (DOD) (dod.defense.gov)
- U.S. Department of Energy (DOE) (www.energy.gov)
- U.S. Department of Health and Human Services (HHS) (www.hhs.gov)
- U.S. Department of the Interior (DOI) (www.doi.gov)
- Center for Domestic Preparedness (cdp.dhs.gov)
- U.S. Department of State (www.state.gov)

- U.S. Department of Transportation (DOT) (www.transportation.gov)
- U.S. Department of the Treasury (home.treasury.gov)
- U.S. Environmental Protection Agency (EPA), Office of Chemical Safety and Pollution Prevention (OCSPP) (www.epa.gov/aboutepa/about-office-chemical-safety-and-pollution-prevention-ocspp)
- Federal Bureau of Investigation (FBI) (www.fbi.gov)
- U.S. Nuclear Regulatory Commission (NRC) (www.nrc.gov)

Agencies under Federal Emergency Management Agency (FEMA) (www.ready.gov)

- National Flood Insurance Program (www.fema.gov/flood-insurance)
- Community Emergency Response Team (www.ready.gov/cert)
- National Response Team (www.nrt.org)
- National Domestic Preparedness Consortium (www.ndpc.us)

- **Non-profits and Other Organizations**
- American Red Cross (www.redcross.org)
- SBP (sbpusa.org)
- Americares (www.americares.org)
- Team Rubicon® (teamrubiconusa.org)
- All Hands and Hearts (www.allhandsandhearts.org)
- Doctors Without Borders (www.doctorswithoutborders.org)
- Direct Relief® (www.directrelief.org)
- REACT International, Inc. (reactintl.org)
- ShelterBox (www.shelterboxusa.org)
- UNICEF (www.unicefusa.org)
- NOVA (www.trynova.org)

Faith-Based Organizations

- The Salvation Army (www.salvationarmyusa.org/usn)
- Volunteers of America® (www.voa.org)
- Samaritan's Purse® (www.samaritanspurse.org)

- NECHAMA Jewish Response to Disaster (nechama.org)
- Children's Disaster Services (www.brethren.org/cds)
- Friends Disaster Services (www.quakersintheworld.org/quakers-in-action/323/Friends-Disaster-Service)
- Catholic Charities USA® (www.catholiccharitiesusa.org)

Made in the USA
Middletown, DE
20 December 2021